c c r
p r e s s

Published by CCR Press
Austin, Texas
www.ccrpress.com

First published 2020
Copy editing by Terry Heller
Design by Kristen Gunn and Dylan Wickstrom

Manufactured in the United States

ISBN 9781734050363

BOSS TEXAS WOMEN

BARBARA JORDAN

Barbara Jordan was born in Houston, Texas, in 1936.

Barbara was an accomplished leader, a powerful writer and commanding public speaker. When she spoke, people listened! In fact, several of her speeches are considered the best speeches in the history of America! She was a Texas State Senator, the first black woman to serve as President pro tempore in the Texas Senate, and the first woman elected to the United States House of Representatives from Texas.

DID YOU KNOW?

As the Texas Senate's president pro tempore, for one day on June 10, 1972, Barbara stepped in as acting governor of Texas.

"WHERE FLOWERS BLOOM, SO DOES HOPE."

LADY BIRD JOHNSON

Claudia Alta "Lady Bird" Johnson was born in Karnack, Texas, in 1912. Lady Bird redefined what it meant to be the First Lady of the United States. She worked directly with Congress to make sure nature, beauty, and native plants and flowers were incorporated into the design of our nation's cities and highways. Lady Bird wanted to make sure that nature was available for everyone.

DID YOU KNOW?

Claudia got her nickname as a small child when a nurse said she was as pretty "as a lady bird."

"THERE ARE THREE TRICKS IN LIFE: HAVE A SENSE OF REAL PURPOSE, A SENSE OF HUMOR, AND A SENSE OF CONSTANT CURIOSITY."

LIZ CARPENTER

Liz Carpenter was born in Salado, Texas, in 1920. Liz was a successful political journalist known for adding humor to political speeches. Liz proved you don't have to be serious to be taken seriously! She became the first newswoman to be press secretary to a First Lady—for Lady Bird Johnson. She also served as Lady Bird Johnson's staff director and wrote speeches for President Lyndon B. Johnson.

DID YOU KNOW?

Liz was often called the "funniest woman in politics."

EMMA TENAYUCA

Emma Tenayuca was born in San Antonio, Texas, in 1916.

Emma saw many of the Mexican laborers in her community being underpaid and working in unsafe conditions. As an activist for these workers she was put in jail and even had to leave San Antonio for a period of time for her own safety! Despite this opposition, Emma persevered. She received a masters degree in education, and spent the rest of her life teaching and inspiring her students.

DID YOU KNOW?

The first record of Emma being arrested for protesting on behalf of workers was when she was only 16 years old!

WENDY DAVIS

Wendy Davis was born in Rhode Island in 1963. Her family moved to Fort Worth, Texas, when she was 10-years-old.

Wendy fights for equal rights for all women. As a single mother, Wendy studied hard and graduated with honors from Harvard Law School. As state senator, Wendy spoke on the senate floor for thirteen hours straight without sitting or going to the bathroom—literally standing to protect the rights of women in Texas!

DID YOU KNOW?

Wendy still has her famous pink sneakers she wore during her filibuster on the senate floor. She plans to give one to each of her granddaughters.

"I DON'T LIKE TO TALK ABOUT THINGS. I LIKE TO FIX THINGS."

ANNISE PARKER

Annise Parker was born in Houston, Texas, in 1956. Annise broke barriers for the gay community and overcame her quiet nature to become an influential leader. As a city council member, Annise was the first openly gay elected offical in Houston. After that, nothing could stop her! She was elected city controller, then later became the first openly gay mayor of a major U.S. city.

DID YOU KNOW?

As a child, Annise's family lovingly nicknamed her "Turtle" because she was so shy. To this day, as an adult, she has a decorative turtle collection!

"DO THE BEST YOU CAN IN EVERY TASK, NO MATTER HOW UNIMPORTANT IT MAY SEEM AT THE TIME."

SANDRA DAY O'CONNOR

Sandra Day O'Connor was born in El Paso, Texas, in 1930. Sandra broke many barriers for women in politics and the judicial court. She was the Attorney General of Arizona, a US Senator, and the first woman to serve as Arizona's floor majority leader. In 1981, she was the first woman to be appointed to the U.S. Supreme Court earning a reputation as a wise and measured judge.

DID YOU KNOW?

While Sandra served on the Supreme Court, she was ranked as one of the most powerful women in the world.

ANGELINA EBERLY

Angelina Eberly was born in Tennessee, in 1798. She moved to Texas in 1825.

Angelina is considered the hero of the Texas Archive War. In 1842, Sam Houston ordered the secret removal of the republic archives from Austin to Houston to make Houston the capital of Texas. Angelina saw what was happening in the middle of the night and fired the large community cannon to wake up people in the town. This saved the archives from being moved, and preserved Austin as the capital city of Texas.

DID YOU KNOW?

Angelina ran several successful inns and taverns in her life. She lived during a time of instability in Texas, but managed to build wealth and become a strong female leader against the odds.

MOLLY IVINS

Molly was born in Monterey, California, in 1944. She moved to Houston, Texas, as a young girl.

Molly used her privilege and razor sharp wit to fight for those who weren't represented in government. Her father was notorious for his strong opinions and bad temper. As Molly grew up, she was drawn to writing and the power of humor to call out corruption. Her experiences sparring with her father inspired a life of speaking truth to power!

DID YOU KNOW?

As an adult, Molly was over 6 feet tall! She credited her height as one of her assets when standing up to powerful politicians.

CHRISTIA ADAIR

Christia Adair was born in Victoria, Texas, in 1893.

Christia was a Black suffragist fighting for and achieving many victories for Black women. In 1923, she fought against a law that said people of color could not vote in Texas Democratic primary elections... and won! However, it was not easy. While Christia fought for Black civil rights, she received bomb threats and other warnings of violence. Christia bravely stood up to these threats, never backing down!

DID YOU KNOW?

Christia helped desegregate many places in Houston. Some of these included city buses, the airport, and the Houston Public Library!

CECILE RICHARDS

Cecile Richards was born in Waco, Texas in 1957.

Cecile believes in "making trouble" for good causes! She's been an activist from her earliest years and has led many influential organizations in Texas. In the 7th grade, Cecile boldly wore an armband protesting the Vietnam War. She was nervous to be the only student speaking out, but she did it anyway! The principal was not happy with her, but her mother was proud. Her mother, Ann Richards, was a schoolteacher who later became the governor of Texas.

DID YOU KNOW?

In 2019, Cecile co-founded the non-profit organization Supermajority to inspire a new generation of women to engage in political activisim, just like her!

ANN RICHARDS

Ann Richards was born in Lakeview, Texas, in 1933.

Ann was a charismatic and powerful speaker! She used her voice to lead, becoming the first woman ever elected governor of Texas based on her merits. Ann was a schoolteacher and mother who loved working on the political campaigns of other Texas women. Governor Ann hired women, people of color, and other under-represented groups to her staff so many voices would be part of the conversation.

DID YOU KNOW?

Despite governing the State of Texas, Ann said that teaching was the hardest work she had ever done.

CASEY CHAPMAN ROSS

CASEY CHAPMAN ROSS is a native and current Austinite, living with her husband and three kids. She earned a BA in Studio Art at the University of Texas and has been a full-time freelance photographer for seven years, focusing on strengthening the efforts of the Democratic Party in Texas. In 2019, she opened CCR Press, a publishing label focusing on progressive titles. As a champion supporting the causes she holds dear, Casey is tireless in her efforts to lift up those causes with positive, powerful imagery.

KRISTEN GUNN

KRISTEN GUNN was born and raised in Houston, Texas. She earned a BA in Film and Digital Media from Baylor University and has worked in film, television, and advertising production for fifteen years. She is also a large-scale outdoor muralist. Some of her immigration murals can be seen around Austin today! She loves using her media and artistic skills to speak for causes she cares about such as immigrants' rights, equality for women and children in foster care. She currently lives in Austin with her two children.

Barbara Jordan
Barbara Jordan:
American Hero,
by Mary Beth Rogers

Learn about how Barbara wrote and delivered a speech that is considered one of the greatest speeches of American History.

Lady Bird Johnson
Lady: The Story of Claudia Alta (Lady Bird) Johnson,
by Jean Flynn
and Liz Carpenter

Learn how Lady Bird Johnson's sense of humor helped her in tough times.

Liz Carpenter
Getting Better All the Time,
by Liz Carpenter

Learn how being from a small town such as Salado gave Liz a "down-to-earth" personality, able to talk comfortably with anyone, whether famous or next door

Emma Tenayuca
That's Not Fair!
by Carmen Tafolla,
Sharyll Tenayuca,
and Celina Marroquin

Learn about Emma growing up, and why being smart and caring about others as a girl made her a great leader in helping many lives.

Wendy Davis
Forgetting to Be Afraid: A Memoir,
by Wendy Davis

Learn how Wendy was able to stand while she talked for 13 hours in defeating a bill!

Christia Adair
Harvard Library: Black Women Oral History Project.
Interviews, 1976-1981. Christia Adair.
OH-31. Schlesinger Library

Learn about Christia and many other Black women, and how even small acts of courage are what can make the difference.

Annise Parker
The Interview: Annise Parker,
by Patrick Michels,
The Texas Observer
(02/16/2016)

Learn about Annise's drive to tackle a problem, take it apart, figure it out, and put a new idea in place.

Sandra Day O'Connor
First: Sandra Day O'Connor,
by Evan Thomas

Learn about how Sandra evolved on issues like LGBTQ rights over her career.

Angelina Eberly
Bartee Haile: Nothing could keep Angelina Eberly down,
By Bartee Haile, The Courier of Montgomery County (08/14/2020)
Quote courtesy of Bartee Haile, This Week in Texas History

Learn why Angelina gave away all her provisions and let the soldiers burn down her house!

Molly Ivins
Molly Ivins: A Rebel Life,
by Molly Ivins

Learn about the famous people, even presidents, who called Molly for advice.

Cecile Richards
Make Trouble, by Cecile Richards

Learn about how Cecile recommends young people get their start in activism.

Ann Richards
Straight from the Heart, by Ann Richards

Learn about memories from girlhood that stayed with her, such as when someone yelled at her during a game: "Make that basket, birdlegs!"

DID YOU KNOW?
You can learn more about these boss women here.

Lightning Source UK Ltd.
Milton Keynes UK
UKHW051442041220
374595UK00004B/69